OWJC
7/11

PLANET EARTH

CAVES

ABDO
Publishing Company

Big
Buddy BOOKS
Planet Earth

Marcia Zappa

VISIT US AT
www.abdopublishing.com

Published by ABDO Publishing Company, 8000 West 78th Street, Edina, Minnesota 55439.

Copyright © 2011 by Abdo Consulting Group, Inc. International copyrights reserved in all countries. No part of this book may be reproduced in any form without written permission from the publisher. Big Buddy Books™ is a trademark and logo of ABDO Publishing Company.

Printed in the United States of America, North Mankato, Minnesota.
032010
092010

 PRINTED ON RECYCLED PAPER

Coordinating Series Editor: Rochelle Baltzer
Contributing Editors: Heidi M.D. Elston, Megan M. Gunderson, BreAnn Rumsch, Sarah Tieck
Graphic Design: Adam Craven
Cover Photograph: *Shutterstock*: John Blanton.
Interior Photographs/Illustrations: *AP Photo*: Vickie Carson/National Park Service (p. 7); *iStockphoto*: ©iStockphoto.com/Cabezonication (p. 29); *Jupiter Images*: Jupiter Images (p. 21), Nancy Nehring ©2008 (p. 21); *NASA* (p. 5); *Peter Arnold, Inc.*: Franco Banfi (p. 19), BIOS (p. 23), ©Biosphoto/Thouvenin Claude (p. 24), Reinhard Divscheri (p. 27), Matt Meadows (p. 25), Wermter, C. (p. 9); *Shutterstock*: aquatic creature (p. 9), Atlaspix (p. 19), John Blanton (p. 20), Horia Bogdan (p. 21), csp (p. 5), Amy Nichole Harris (p. 17), jeff gynane (p. 30), Juice Team (p. 5), Anton Kossmann (p. 5), Jaan-Martin Kuusmann (p. 9), Ales Liska (p. 13), Andre Nantel (p. 15), Jason L. Price (p. 21), Tobik (p. 11).

Library of Congress Cataloging-in-Publication Data

Zappa, Marcia, 1985-
  Caves / Marcia Zappa.
    p. cm. -- (Planet earth)
  ISBN 978-1-61613-490-7
  1. Caves--Juvenile literature. I. Title.
  GB601.2.Z37 2011
  551.44'7--dc22
                        2009053193

TABLE OF CONTENTS

A LOOK BELOW

Earth has many types of landforms. These include mountains, hills, and valleys. Caves are landforms, too. They are hidden underground.

A cave is a hole in Earth's surface. Caves occur naturally. They provide homes for many animals. People like to study and explore these interesting, beautiful landforms.

Many caves are filled with rock formations. Some even have lakes, rivers, and waterfalls!

ALL SHAPES AND SIZES

Caves exist in many shapes and sizes. Some caves are simple. They may have only one small room, or chamber.

Other caves have several chambers. Some caves have tunnels that spread out for miles!

Kentucky's Mammoth-Flint Ridge cave system is about 340 miles (550 km) long. It is the longest cave that has ever been explored.

There are many different types of caves. Scientists group them based on how they form. The most common groups include solution caves, lava tubes, and sea caves.

Solution caves (*left*) and sea caves (*below left*) form from old rock. Lava tubes (*below*) form from new rock.

9

EATEN AWAY

Solution caves form when a liquid slowly dissolves rock. Most solution caves are created by weak acids. Acids form when water mixes with certain chemicals. These liquid solutions cause chemical reactions that dissolve rock.

Solution caves are commonly found in soft rock, such as limestone.

SCIENCE SPOT

Solution caves are named for the word *solution*. A solution is a mixture that forms when something is dissolved into a liquid.

To form a cave, an acid solution flows down through tiny cracks in rock and soil. It eats away the rock.

Over time, rooms and tunnels form underground. The acid solution flows out of these spaces. It leaves behind a solution cave.

Solution caves form over thousands of years.

13

BURNING UP!

Lava tubes form from magma. Magma, or lava, is rock that is so hot it is melted. It forms deep inside Earth. Magma can reach Earth's surface through deep cracks. Or, it can erupt from volcanoes.

Lava tubes form throughout the world. They are most common in areas with lots of volcanoes. These include Hawaii, Italy, and Japan.

When magma reaches Earth's surface, it spreads out and flows over land. Sometimes, its outer surface cools and hardens while its center remains melted.

The magma in the center continues to flow. After a while, it drains out. The magma leaves behind its hard outer shell, known as a lava tube.

Lava tubes form near Earth's surface. Thin, holey roofs are a common feature.

IN WITH THE TIDE

A sea cave forms when ocean waves crash against a cliff. Sometimes waves hit a weak spot, such as soft rock or a crack.

The waves pound away at the weak spot, wearing away rock. This causes a hole to form in the cliff. Over time, the hole can grow into a sea cave.

Many people explore sea caves by scuba diving. Scuba divers use special gear so they can breathe and see underwater.

Sea caves most often form in soft rock, such as sandstone or limestone.

19

STALACTITES

NATURE'S SCULPTURES

Many interesting rock formations exist inside caves. After a cave forms, moving water continues to dissolve rock. It deposits bits of dissolved rock called minerals in new locations. Often, minerals join together to make formations.

STALAGMITES

Stalagmites form up from a cave's floor. They are created when water and minerals drip off a cave's ceiling.

When stalactites and stalagmites grow together, they can form columns.

COLUMNS

Draperies are thin sheets of rock. They hang from a cave's ceiling or wall. Striped draperies are sometimes called cave bacon!

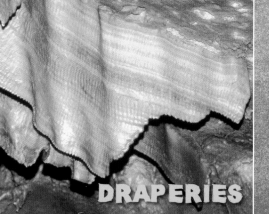

Flowstones form when water flows over the walls or floor of a cave. Many people think flowstones look like frozen waterfalls.

DRAPERIES

FLOWSTONES

LIFE IN CAVES

Caves are important to life on Earth. Thousands of years ago, humans known as cave dwellers lived in caves. Today, people explore caves as a hobby. This activity is known as caving or spelunking.

SCIENCE SPOT

The scientific study of caves is called speleology. Speleologists are the scientists who study caves.

Tools and paintings found in caves teach scientists how cave dwellers lived.

SCIENCE SPOT

Some plants grow in caves. Ferns and mosses grow near cave entrances, where they can get some sunlight.

Caves also provide homes for animals. These include bears, raccoons, bats, birds, salamanders, and bugs. Most of these animals leave caves to find food. They return to sleep.

Other animals spend their whole lives in caves. These are called troglobites. They include special types of beetles, fish, and lizards. Troglobites live where there is no light or changing weather. They are often blind and have thin, colorless skin.

Troglobites are specially suited to living in caves. Many cannot survive above ground.

PROTECTING CAVES

Caves are natural wonders. Many people study and **explore** them.

Sometimes people harm caves. They may break a cave's natural **formations**. Or, they may hurt its plants and animals by mistake.

SCIENCE SPOT

Sometimes people bring harmful chemicals into caves. For example, sunscreen is made from chemicals. It can get into a cave's water supply and harm the cave's walls.

Cavers wear headlamps and carry flashlights to see their way around.

Some people work to **protect** caves. Careful cavers try to leave caves the way they found them. You can help too! Never enter a cave alone. Only **explore** caves with knowledgeable cavers. And be careful not to harm cave **formations** or wildlife. This helps keep caves a beautiful part of planet Earth!

Caves are one of Earth's many natural wonders!

DOWN TO EARTH:
A FEW MORE FACTS ABOUT CAVES

- Some caves form in huge mounds of ice called glaciers. Glacier caves may have rock floors and ice walls and roofs.
- Caves are not used to the light, gases, and other elements on Earth's surface. So, they can easily be harmed when people explore them.
- Many caves form when limestone dissolves (*right*). Some limestone areas contain many sinkholes, underground streams, and caves. These areas are known as karsts.

IMPORTANT WORDS

chemical (KEH-mih-kuhl) a substance that can cause reactions and changes.

deposit to let fall or sink.

dissolve (dih-ZAHLV) to become part of a liquid.

explore to go into in order to make a discovery or to have an adventure.

formation something that has been formed into a shape.

landform a natural feature of a land surface. Hills and mountains are types of landforms.

mineral a natural substance. Minerals make up rocks and other parts of nature.

protect (pruh-TEHKT) to guard against harm or danger.

volcano a mountain from which hot liquid rock or steam come out.

WEB SITES

To learn more about caves, visit ABDO Publishing Company online. Web sites about caves are featured on our Book Links page. These links are routinely monitored and updated to provide the most current information available.

www.abdopublishing.com

INDEX